The Mueller Report's:
Appendix A, B, C, & D

(Introduction by TG Fugate, author of Verbal SnapShots for the UpScale Privy— Volumes 1, 2, & 3)

The Appendix of *The Mueller Report*, some may argue, is as most anyone would expect — rather bland at best. Surprise, surprise there is an important exception in this circumstance. While Sections A, B, and D are perhaps typical Appendix material, the 23 pages of fine print that's found in Appendix C (several of which are duplicated questions) is a copy of the written questions (and the President's answers) that were submitted to Donald J. Trump by the Office of the Special Council following more than a year long effort to reach an agreement to interview the President face to face on topics relevant to both Russian-election interference during the 2016 Presidential election and the possible obstruction-of-justice that occurred thereafter by the sitting US President (Donald J. Trump).

If you are simply too busy to find the time to read the 448 pages of fine print contained within *The Mueller Report* as was presented by US Attorney General, William P Barr, do yourself a favor and read at a minimum, Appendix C of this relatively small publication.

While a personal interview never occurred with the President, the written questions and most particularly the answers contained within Appendix C may surprise you.

No one is likely to deny that given the opportunity, US President Trump, boasts mightily of his ability to recall past events and or statements he has previously made and or experienced . . . The number of times he has professed to have an outstanding memory? . . No-one seems to recall! Still, on any day of the week, the President often claims to have *"one of the all-time great memories"*! Yet, he has proven a tendency over a number of years to lose his "great recollection ability" when in court or under oath. And too, he seems to suffer bouts of amnesia when it comes to recalling recent comments; past unsavory actions; or the number of strokes he has "played" during golf games with his opponent(s).

Perhaps, the Presidents phenomenal, self-professed, recollection ability was never more important than when he agreed to provide correct and precise answers (under oath) to each of 5 question submitted to him and his personal attorneys by Special Investigator Robert S Mueller which is now "Appendix C" of *The Mueller Report*; a huge document recently (4-18-2019) placed into the Public Domain by US Attorney General, William Pelham Barr.

In an effort to lend impartiality to the questions submitted to the President, it should be noted that 4 of the 5 questions submitted contain multiple parts; therefore, their were actually a couple dozen questions. Yet, upon completing his "test" questions, the President declared: *"I answered them very easily."*

Until the the release of *The Mueller Report*, you could only guess at the actual volume and level of difficulty the questions that were submitted held . . . Now you can make that determination yourself!

Regardless, within this publication, Appendix A, B, & and D are merely copies borrowed from the original Mueller Report — except, the font size has been converted to easy on the eyes large print. While Appendix C has likewise been converted to large print, each question is followed by the answer given . . . Unlike the original document, wherein all the questions first appear and are then followed by the answers several pages later.

In regard to "editing" of the following Appendix documents, the occasional topographical errors and omissions remain as was originally submitted by US Attorney General

William P Barr in an effort to reflect the authenticity of the document. However, the text has been converted from fine text to large print for your reading convenience. In addition, when feasible, an effort has been made to "group" and underline reference data and or documentation source(s) located between sentences that may first appear to be incomplete; the intent is to provide a better reading flow and to avoid the possibility of confusion — a convenience not provided in the original Mueller Report's publication . . .

Finally, The Mueller Report, including the Appendix documents (A, B, C, & D) that follow are also available within the Public Domain. The documents herein were released by the US Department of Justice (04-18-2019); hence no copyright is claimed. The original publication can be viewed in fine print at:

https://www.justice.gov/storage/report.pdf

Appendix A, B, C, & D for the Report On the

Investigation Into Russian Interference In The 2016 Presidential Election

By Special Counsel Robert S. Mueller, III

Submitted Pursuant to 28 C.F.R. § 600.8(c)

Washington, D.C.

March 2019

Appendix A, B, C, & D
Directory

Appendix A

Office of the Deputy Attorney General

Washington, D.U. 20530 ONE NRC

ORDER NO. 3915-2017

APPOINTMENT OF SPECIAL COUNSEL

TO INVESTIGATE RUSSIAN INTERFERENCE WITH

THE 2016 PRESIDENTIAL ELECTION AND RELATED MATTERS

By virtue of the authority vested in me as Acting Attorney General, including 28 U.S.C. §§ 509, 510, and 515, in order to discharge my responsibility to provide supervision and management of the Department of Justice, and to ensure a full and thorough investigation of the Russian government's efforts to interfere in the 2016 presidential election, I hereby order as follows:

(a) Robert S. Mueller III is appointed to serve as Special Counsel for the United States Department of Justice.

(b) The Special Counsel is authorized to conduct the investigation continued by then-FBI Director James B. Comey in testimony before the House Permanent Select Committee on Intelligence on March 20,2017, including:

(i) any links and/or coordination between the Russian government and individuals associated with the campaign of President Donald Trump; and

(ii) any matters that arose or may arise directly from the investigation; and

(iii) any other matters within the scope of 28 C.F.R. § 600.4(a).

(c If the Special Counsel believes it is necessary and appropriate, the Special Counsel is authorized to prosecute federal crimes arising from the investigation of these matters.

(c) Sections 600.4 through 600.10 of Title 28 of the Code of Federal Regulations are applicable to the Special Counsel.

5/17/17
Date

Rod J. Rosenstein
Acting Attorney General

Appendix B

APPENDIX B: GLOSSARY

The following glossary contains names and brief descriptions of individuals and entities referenced in the two volumes of this report. It is not intended to be comprehensive and is intended only to assist a reader in the reading the rest of the report.

Agalarov, Emin . . . Performer, executive vice president of Crocus Group, and son of Aras Agalarov; helped arrange the June 9, 2016 meeting at Trump Tower between Natalia Veselnitskaya and Trump Campaign officials.

Akhmetov, Rinat . . . Former member in the Ukrainian parliament who hired Paul Manafort to conduct work for Ukrainian political party, the Party of Regions.

Akhmetshin, Rinat . . . U.S. lobbyist and associate of Natalia Veselnitskaya who attended the June 9, 2016 meeting at Trump Tower between Veselnitskaya and Trump Campaign officials.

Aslanov, Dzheykhun (Jay) . . . Head of U.S. department of the Internet Research Agency, which engaged in an "active measures" social media campaign to interfere in the 2016 U.S. presidential election.

Assange, Julian . . . Founder of WikiLeaks, which in 2016 posted on the internet documents stolen from entities and individuals affiliated with the Democratic Party.

Aven, Petr . . . Chairman of the board of Alfa-Bank who attempted outreach to the Presidential Transition Team in connection with anticipated post-election sanctions.

Bannon, Stephen (Steve) . . . White House chief strategist and senior counselor to President Trump (Jan. 2017 – Aug. 2017); chief executive of the Trump Campaign.

Baranov, Andrey . . . Director of investor relations at Russian state-owned oil company, Rosneft, and associate of Carter Page.

Berkowitz, Avi . . . Assistant to Jared Kushner.

Boente, Dana . . . Acting Attorney General (Jan. 2017 - Feb. 2017); Acting Deputy Attorney General (Feb. 2017 – Apr. 2017).

Bogacheva, Anna . . . Internet Research Agency employee who worked on "active measures" social media campaign to interfere in in the 2016 U.S. presidential election; traveled to the United States under false pretenses in 2014.

Bossert, Thomas (Tom) . . . Former homeland security advisor to the President who also served as a senior official on the Presidential Transition Team.

Boyarkin, Viktor . . . Employee of Russian oligarch Oleg Deripaska.

Boyd, Charles . . . Chairman of the board of directors at the Center for the National Interest, a U.S.-based think tank with operations in and connections to Russia.

Boyko, Yuriy . . . Member of the Ukrainian political party Opposition Bloc and member of the Ukrainian parliament.

Brand, Rachel . . . Associate Attorney General (May 2017 - Feb. 2018).

Browder, William (Bill) . . . Founder of Hermitage Capital Management who lobbied in favor of the Magnitsky Act, which imposed financial and travel sanctions on Russian officials.

Bulatov, Alexander . . . Russian intelligence official who associated with Carter Page in 2008.

Burchik, Mikhail . . . Executive director of the Internet Research Agency, which engaged in an "active measures" social media campaign to interfere in the 2016 U.S. presidential election.

Burck, William . . . Personal attorney to Don McGahn, White House Counsel.

Burnham, James . . . Attorney in the White House Counsel's Office who attended January 2017 meetings between Sally Yates and Donald McGahn.

Burt, Richard . . . Former U.S. ambassador who had done work Alfa-Bank and was a board member of the Center for the National Interest.

Bystrov, Mikhail . . . General director of the Internet Research Agency, which engaged in an "active measures" social media campaign to interfere in the 2016 U.S. presidential election.

Calamari, Matt . . . Chief operating officer for the Trump Organization.

Caputo, Michael . . . Trump Campaign advisor.

Chaika, Yuri . . . Prosecutor general of the Russian Federation who also maintained a relationship with Aras Agalarov.

Christie, Chris . . . Former Governor of New Jersey.

Clapper, James . . . Director of National Intelligence (Aug. 2010 – Jan. 2017).

Clovis, Samuel Jr. . . . Chief policy advisor and national co-chair of the Trump Campaign.

Coats, Dan . . . Director of National Intelligence.

Cobb, Ty . . . Special Counsel to the President (July 2017 – May 2018).

Cohen, Michael . . . Former vice president to the Trump Organization and special counsel to Donald Trump who spearheaded an effort to build a Trump-branded property in Moscow. He admitted to lying to Congress about the project.

Comey, James Jr. . . . Director of the Federal Bureau of Investigation (Sept. 4, 2013 - May 9, 2017).

Conway, Kellyanne . . . Counselor to President Trump and manager of the Trump Campaign.

Corallo, Mark . . . Spokesman for President Trump's personal legal team (June 2017 - July 2017).

Corsi, Jerome . . . Author and political commentator who formerly worked for WorldNet Daily and Info Wars.

██

██

████████████████████████████████████

Costello, Robert . . . Attorney who represented he had a close relationship with Rudolph Giuliani, the President's personal counsel.

Credico, Randolph (Randy) . . . Radio talk show host who interviewed Julian Assange in 2016.

██

██

██

████████████████████████████████████

Davis, Richard (Rick) Jr. . . . Partner with Pegasus Sustainable Century Merchant Bank, business partner of Paul Manafort, and co-founder of the Davis Manafort lobbying firm.

Dearborn, Rick . . .Former White House deputy chief of staff for policy who previously served as chief of staff to Senator Jeff Sessions.

Dempsey, Michael . . . Office of Director of National Intelligence official who recalled discussions with Dan Coats after Coats's meeting with President Trump on March 22, 2017.

Denman, Diana . . . Delegate to 2016 Republican National Convention who proposed a platform plank amendment that included armed support for Ukraine.

Deripaska, Oleg . . . Russian businessman with ties to Vladimir Putin who hired Paul Manafort for consulting work between 2005 and 2009.

Dhillon, Uttam . . . Attorney in the White House Counsel's Office (Jan. 2017 – June 2018).

Dmitriev, Kirill . . . Head of the Russian Direct Investment Fund (RDIF); met with Erik Prince in the Seychelles in January 2017 and, separately, drafted a U.S.-Russia reconciliation plan with Rick Gerson.

Donaldson, Annie . . . Chief of staff to White House Counsel Donald McGahn (Jan. 2017 - Dec. 2018).

Dvorkovich, Arkady . . . Deputy prime minister of the Russian Federation and chairman of the board of directors of the New Economic School in Moscow. He met with Carter Page twice in 2016.

Dvoskin, Evgeney . . . Executive of Genbank in Crimea and associate of Felix Sater.

Eisenberg, John . . . Attorney in the White House Counsel's Office and legal counsel for the National Security Council.

Erchova, Lana (a/k/a Lana Alexander) . . . Ex-wife of Dmitry Klokov who emailed Ivanka Trump to introduce Klokov to the Trump Campaign in the fall of 2015.

Fabrizio, Anthony (Tony) . . . Partner at the research and consulting firm Fabrizio, Lee & Associates. He was a pollster for the Trump Campaign and worked with Paul Manafort on Ukraine-related polling after the election.

Fishbein, Jason . . . Attorney who performed worked for Julian Assange and also sent WikiLeaks a password for an unlaunched website Putin Trump.org on September 20, 2016.

Flynn, Michael G. (a/k/a Michael Flynn Jr.) . . . Son of Michael T. Flynn

Flynn, Michael T. . . . National Security Advisor (Jan. 20, 2017 - Feb. 13, 2017), Director of the Defense Intelligence Agency (July 2012 - Aug. 7, 2014), and Trump Campaign advisor. He pleaded guilty to lying to the FBI about communications with Ambassador Sergey Kislyak in December 2016.

Foresman, Robert (Bob) . . . Investment banker who sought meetings with the Trump Campaign in spring 2016 to discuss Russian foreign policy, and after the election met with Michael Flynn.

Futerfas, Alan . . . Outside counsel for the Trump Organization and subsequently personal counsel for Donald Trump Jr.

Garten, Alan . . . General counsel of the Trump Organization.

Gates, Richard (Rick) III . . . Deputy campaign manager for Trump Campaign, Trump Inaugural Committee deputy chairman, and longtime employee of Paul Manafort. He pleaded guilty to conspiring to defraud the United States and violate U.S. laws, as well as making false statements to the FBI.

Gerson, Richard (Rick) . . . New York hedge fund manager and associate of Jared Kushner. During the transition period, he worked with Kirill Dmitriev on a proposal for reconciliation between the United States and Russia.

Gistaro, Edward . . . Deputy Director of National Intelligence for Intelligence Integration.

Glassner, Michael . . . Political director of the Trump Campaign who helped introduce George Papadopoulos to others in the Trump Campaign.

Goldstone, Robert . . . Publicist for Emin Agalarov who contacted Donald Trump Jr. to arrange the June 9, 2016 meeting at Trump Tower between Natalia Veselnitskaya and Trump Campaign officials.

Gordon, Jeffrey (J.D.) . . . National security advisor to the Trump Campaign involved in changes to the Republican party platform and who communicated with Russian Ambassador Sergey Kislyak at the Republican National Convention.

Gorkov, Sergey . . . Chairman of Vnesheconombank (VEB), a Russian state-owned bank, who met with Jared Kushner during the transition period.

Graff, Rhona . . . Senior vice-president and executive assistant to Donald J. Trump at the Trump Organization.

Hawker, Jonathan . . . Public relations consultant at FTI Consulting; worked with Davis Manafort International LLC on public relations campaign in Ukraine.

Heilbrunn, Jacob , . . Editor of the National Interest, the periodical that officially hosted candidate Trump's April 2016 foreign policy speech.

Hicks, Hope . . .White House communications director (Aug. 2017 – Mar. 2018) and press secretary for the Trump Campaign.

Holt, Lester . . . NBC News anchor who interviewed President Trump on May 11, 2017.

Hunt, Jody . . . Chief of staff to Attorney General Jeff Sessions (Feb. 2017 - Oct. 2017).

Ivanov, Igor . . . President of the Russian International Affairs Council and former Russian foreign minister. Ivan Timofeev told George Papadopoulos that Ivanov advised on arranging a "Moscow visit" for the Trump Campaign.

Ivanov, Sergei . . . Special representative of Vladimir Putin, former Russian deputy prime minister, and former FSB deputy director. In January 2016, Michael Cohen emailed the Kremlin requesting to speak to Ivanov.

Kasowitz, Marc . . . President Trump's personal counsel (May 2017 – July 2017).

Katsyv, Denis . . . Son of Peter Katsyv; owner of Russian company Prevezon Holdings Ltd. and associate of Natalia Veselnitskaya.

Katsyv, Peter . . . Russian businessman and father of Denis Katsyv.

Kaveladze, Irakli (Ike) . . . Vice president at Crocus Group and Aras Agalarov's deputy in the United States. He participated in the June 9, 2016 meeting at Trump Tower between Natalia Veselnitskaya and Trump Campaign officials.

Kaverzina, Irina . . . Employee of the Internet Research Agency, which engaged in an "active measures" social media campaign to interfere in the 2016 U.S. presidential election.

Kelly, John . . . White House chief of staff (July 2017 – Jan. 2019).

Khalilzad, Zalmay . . . U.S. special representative to Afghanistan and former U.S. ambassador. He met with Senator Jeff Sessions during foreign policy dinners put together through the Center for the National Interest.

Kilimnik, Konstantin . . . Russian-Ukrainian political consultant and long-time employee of Paul Manafort assessed by the FBI to have ties to Russian intelligence.

Kislyak, Sergey . . . Former Russian ambassador to the United States and current Russian senator from Mordovia.

Klimentov, Denis . . . Employee of the New Economic School who informed high-ranking Russian government officials of Carter Page's July 2016 visit to Moscow.

Klimentov, Dmitri . . . Brother of Denis Klimentov who contacted Kremlin press secretary Dmitri Peskov about Carter Page's July 2016 visit to Moscow.

Klokov, Dmitry . . . Executive for PJSC Federal Grid Company of Unified Energy System and former aide to Russia's minister of energy. He communicated with Michael Cohen about a possible meeting between Vladimir Putin and candidate Trump.

Kobyakov, Anton . . . Advisor to Vladimir Putin and member of the Roscongress Foundation who invited candidate Trump to the St. Petersburg International Economic Forum.

Krickovic, Andrej . . . Professor at the Higher School of Economics who recommended that Carter Page give a July 2016 commencement address in Moscow.

Krylova, Aleksandra . . . Internet Research Agency employee who worked on "active measures" social media campaign to interfere in the 2016 U.S. presidential election; traveled to the United States under false pretenses in 2014.

Kushner, Jared . . . President Trump's son-in-law and senior advisor to the President.

Kuznetsov, Sergey . . . Russian government official at the Russian Embassy to the United States who transmitted Vladimir Putin's congratulations to President-Elect Trump for his electoral victory on November 9, 2016.

Landrum, Pete . . . Advisor to Senator Jeff Sessions who attended the September 2016 meeting between Sessions and Russian Ambassador Sergey Kislyak.

Lavrov, Sergey . . . Russian minister of foreign affairs and former permanent representative of Russia to the United Nations.

Ledeen, Barbara . . . Senate staffer and associate of Michael Flynn who sought to obtain Hillary Clinton emails during the 2016 U.S. presidential campaign period.

Ledeen, Michael . . . Member of the Presidential Transition Team who advised on foreign policy and national security matters.

Ledgett, Richard . . . Deputy director of the National Security Agency (Jan. 2014 - Apr, 2017); present when President Trump called Michael Rogers on March 26, 2017.

Lewandowski, Corey . . . Campaign manager for the Trump Campaign (Jan. 2015 – June 2016).

Luff, Sandra . . . Legislative director for Senator Jeff Sessions; attended a September 2016 meeting between Sessions and Russian Ambassador Sergey Kislyak.

Lyovochkin, Serhiy . . . Member of Ukrainian parliament and member of Ukrainian political party, Opposition Bloc Party.

Magnitsky, Sergei . . . Russian tax specialist who alleged Russian government corruption and died in Russian police custody in 2009. His death prompted passage of the Magnitsky Act, which imposed financial and travel sanctions on Russian officials.

Malloch, Theodore (Ted) . . . Chief executive officer of Global Fiduciary Governance and the Roosevelt Group. He was a London-based associate of Jerome Corsi.

Manafort, Paul Jr. . . . Trump campaign member (March 2016 – Aug. 2016) and chairman and chief strategist (May 2016 – Aug. 2016).

Mashburn, John . . . Trump administration official and former policy director to the Trump Campaign.

McCabe, Andrew . . . Acting director of the FBI (May 2017 – Aug. 2017); deputy director of the FBI (Feb. 2016 - Jan. 2018).

McCord, Mary . . . Acting Assistant Attorney General (Oct. 2016 – May 2017).

McFarland, Kathleen (K.T.) . . . Deputy White House National Security Advisor (Jan. 2017 - May 2017).

McGahn, Donald (Don) . . . White House Counsel (Jan. 2017 - Oct. 2018).

Medvedev, Dmitry . . . Prime Minister of Russia.

Melnik, Yuriy . . . Spokesperson for the Russian Embassy in Washington, D.C., who connected with George Papadopoulos on social media.

Mifsud, Joseph . . . Maltese national and former London-based professor who, immediately after returning from Moscow in April 2016, told George Papadopoulos that the Russians had "dirt" in the form of thousands of Clinton emails.

B-14

Miller, Matt . . . Trump Campaign staff member who was present at the meeting of the National Security and Defense Platform Subcommittee in July 2016.

Miller, Stephen . . . Senior advisor to the President.

Millian, Sergei . . . Founder of the Russian American Chamber of Commerce who met with George Papadopoulos during the campaign.

Mnuchin, Steven . . . Secretary of the Treasury.

████████████

████████████████████

██████████

Müller-Maguhn, Andrew . . .Member of hacker association Chaos Computer Club and associate of Julian Assange, founder of WikiLeaks.

Nader, George . . . Advisor to the United Arab Emirates's Crown Prince who arranged a meeting between Kirill Dmitriev and Erik Prince during the transition period.

Netyksho, Viktor . . . Russian military officer in command of a unit involved in Russian hack-and-release operations to interfere in the 2016 U.S. presidential election.

Oganov, Georgiy . . . Advisor to Oleg Deripaska and a board member of investment company Basic Element. He met with Paul Manafort in Spain in early 2017.

Oknyansky, Henry (a/k/a Henry Greenberg) . . . Florida-based Russian individual who claimed to have derogatory information pertaining to Hillary Clinton. He met with Roger Stone in May 2016.

Page, Carter . . . Foreign policy advisor to the Trump Campaign who advocated pro-Russian views and made July 2016 and December 2016 visits to Moscow.

Papadopoulos, George . . . Foreign policy advisor to the Trump Campaign who received information from Joseph Mifsud that Russians had "dirt" in the form of thousands of Clinton emails. He pleaded guilty to lying to the FBI about his contact with Mifsud.

Parscale, Bradley . . . Digital media director for the 2016 Trump Campaign.

Patten, William (Sam) Jr. . . . . Lobbyist and business partner of Konstantin Kilimnik.

Peskov, Dmitry . . . Deputy chief of staff of and press secretary for the Russian presidential administration.

Phares, Walid . . . Foreign policy advisor to the Trump Campaign and co-secretary general of the Transatlantic Parliamentary Group on Counterterrorism (TAG).

Pinedo, Richard . . . U.S. person who pleaded guilty to a single-count information of identity fraud.

Podesta, John Jr. . . . . Clinton campaign chairman whose email account was hacked by the GRU. WikiLeaks released his stolen emails during the 2016 campaign.

Podobnyy, Victor . . . Russian intelligence officer who interacted with Carter Page while operating inside the United

States; later charged in 2015 with conspiring to act as an unregistered agent of Russia.

Poliakova, Elena . . . Personal assistant to Dmitry Peskov who responded to Michael Cohen's outreach about the Trump Tower Moscow project in January 2016.

Polonskaya, Olga . . . Russian national introduced to George Papadopoulos by Joseph Mifsud as an individual with connections to Vladimir Putin.

Pompeo, Michael . . . U.S. Secretary of State; director of the Central Intelligence Agency (Jan. 2017 - Apr. 2018).

Porter, Robert . . . White House staff secretary (Jan. 2017 - Feb. 2018).

Priebus, Reince . . . White House chief of staff (Jan. 2017 - July 2017); chair of the Republican National Committee (Jan. 2011 - Jan. 2017).

Prigozhin, Yevgeniy . . . Head of Russian companies Concord Catering and Concord Management and Consulting; supported and financed the Internet Research Agency, which engaged in an "active measures" social media campaign to interfere in the 2016 U.S. presidential election.

Prikhodko, Sergei . . . First deputy head of the Russian Government Office and former Russian deputy prime minister. In January 2016, he invited candidate Trump to the St. Petersburg International Economic Forum.

Prince, Erik . . . Businessman and Trump Campaign supporter who met with Presidential Transition Team officials after the election and traveled to the Seychelles to meet with Kirill Dmitriev in January 2017.

Raffel, Josh . . . White House communications advisor (Apr. 2017 - Feb. 2018).

Rasin, Alexei . . . Ukrainian associate of Henry Oknyansky who claimed to possess derogatory information regarding Hillary Clinton.

Rogers, Michael . . . Director of the National Security Agency (Apr. 2014 - May 2018).

Rosenstein, Rod . . . Deputy Attorney General (Apr. 2017-present); Acting Attorney General for the Russian election interference investigation (May 2017 - Nov. 2018).

Rozov, Andrei . . . Chairman of I.C. Expert Investment Company, a Russian real-estate development corporation that signed a letter of intent for the Trump Tower Moscow project in 2015.

Rtskhiladze, Giorgi . . . Executive of the Silk Road Transatlantic Alliance, LLC who communicated with Cohen about a Trump Tower Moscow proposal.

Ruddy, Christopher . . . Chief executive of Newsmax Media and associate of President Trump.

Rybicki, James . . . FBI chief of staff (May 2015 - Feb. 2018).

Samochornov, Anatoli . . . Translator who worked with Natalia Veselnitskaya and attended a June 9, 2016 meeting at Trump Tower between Veselnitskaya and Trump Campaign officials.

Sanders, Sarah Huckabee . . . White House press secretary (July 2017 - present).

Sater, Felix . . . Real-estate advisor who worked with Michael Cohen to pursue a Trump Tower Moscow project.

Saunders, Paul J. . . . Executive with the Center for the National Interest who worked on outlines and logistics of candidate Trump's April 2016 foreign policy speech.

Sechin, Igor . . . Executive chairman of Rosneft, a Russian-stated owned oil company.

Sessions, Jefferson . . . Attorney General (Feb. 2017 – Nov. 2018); U.S. Senator (Jan. 1997 – III (Jeff) Feb. 2017); head of the Trump Campaign's foreign policy advisory team.

Shoygu, Sergey . . . Russian Minister of Defense.

Simes, Dimitri . . . President and chief executive officer of the Center for the National Interest.

Smith, Peter . . . Investment banker active in Republican politics who sought to obtain Hillary Clinton emails during the 2016 U.S. presidential campaign period.

Spicer, Sean . . . White House press secretary and communications director (Jan. 2017 – July 2017).

Stone, Roger . . . Advisor to the Trump Campaign

Tillerson, Rex . . . U.S. Secretary of State (Feb. 2017 - Mar. 2018).

Timofeev, Ivan . . . Director of programs at the Russian International Affairs Council and program director of the Valdai Discussion Club who communicated in 2016 with George Papadopoulos, attempting to arrange a meeting between the Russian government and the Trump Campaign.

Trump, Donald Jr. . . . President Trump's son; trustee and executive vice president of the Trump Organization; helped arrange and attended the June 9, 2016 meeting at Trump Tower between Natalia Veselnitskaya and Trump Campaign officials.

Trump, Eric . . . President Trump's son; trustee and executive vice president of the Trump Organization.

Trump, Ivanka . . . President Trump's daughter; advisor to the President and former executive vice president of the Trump Organization.

Ushakov, Yuri Viktorovich . . . Aide to Vladimir Putin and former Russian ambassador to the United States; identified to the Presidential Transition Team as the proposed channel to the Russian government.

Vaino, Anton . . . Chief of staff to Russian president Vladimir Putin.

Van der Zwaan, Alexander . . . Former attorney at Skadden, Arps, Slate, Meagher & Flom, LLP; worked with Paul Manafort and Rick Gates. Vargas, Catherine Executive assistant to Jared Kushner.

Vasilchenko, Gleb . . . Internet Research Agency employee who engaged in an "active measures" social media campaign to interfere in the 2016 U.S. presidential election.

Veselnitskaya, Natalia . . . Russian attorney who advocated for the repeal of the Magnitsky Act and was the principal speaker at the June 9, 2016 meeting at Trump Tower with Trump Campaign officials.

Weber, Shlomo . . . Rector of the New Economic School (NES) in Moscow who invited Carter Page to speak at NES commencement in July 2016.

Yanukovych, Viktor . . . Former president of Ukraine who had worked with Paul Manafort.

Yates, Sally . . . Acting Attorney General (Jan. 20, 2017 – Jan. 30, 2017); Deputy Attorney General (Jan. 10, 2015 - Jan. 30, 2017).

Yatsenko, Sergey . . . Deputy chief financial officer of Gazprom, a Russian state-owned energy company, and associate of Carter Page.

Zakharova, Maria . . . Director of the Russian Ministry of Foreign Affair's Information and Press Department who received notification of Carter Page's speech in July 2016 from Denis Klimentov.

Zayed al Nahyan, Mohammed bin . . . Crown Prince of Abu Dhabi and deputy supreme commander of the United Arab Emirates (UAE) armed forces.

Entities and Organizations

Alfa-Bank . . . Russia's largest commercial bank, which is headed by Petr Aven.

Center for the National Interest (CNI) . . . U.S.-based think tank with expertise in and connections to Russia. CNI's publication, the National Interest, hosted candidate Trump's foreign policy speech in April 2016.

Concord . . . Umbrella term for Concord Management and Consulting, LLC and Concord Catering, which are Russian companies controlled by Yevgeniy Prigozhin.

Crocus Group or Crocus International . . . A Russian real-estate and property development company that, in 2013, hosted the Miss Universe Pageant, and from 2013 through 2014, worked with the Trump Organization on a Trump Moscow project.

DCLeaks . . . Fictitious online persona operated by the GRU that released stolen documents during the 2016 U.S. presidential campaign period.

Democratic Congressional Campaign Committee . . . Political committee working to elect Democrats to the House of Representatives; hacked by the GRU in April 2016.

Democratic National Committee . . . Formal governing body for the Democratic Party; hacked by the GRU in April 2016.

Duma . . . Lower House of the national legislature of the Russian Federation.

Gazprom . . . Russian oil and gas company majority-owned by the Russian government.

Global Energy Capital, LLC . . . Investment and management firm founded by Carter Page.

Global Partners in Diplomacy . . . Event hosted in partnership with the U.S. Department of State and the Republican National Convention. In 2016, Jeff Sessions and J.D. Gordon delivered speeches at the event and interacted with Russian Ambassador Sergey Kislyak.

Guccifer 2.0 . . . Fictitious online persona operated by the GRU that released stolen documents during the 2016 U.S. presidential campaign period.

I.C. Expert Investment Company . . . Russian real-estate and development corporation that signed a letter of intent with a Trump Organization subsidiary to develop a Trump Moscow property.

Internet Research Agency (IRA) . . . Russian entity based in Saint Petersburg and funded by Concord that engaged in an "active measures" social media campaign to interfere in the 2016 U.S. presidential election.

KLS Research LLC . . . Business established by an associate of and at the direction of Peter Smith to further Smith's search for Hillary Clinton emails.

Kremlin . . . Official residence of the president of the Russian Federation; it is used colloquially to refer to the office of the president or the Russian government.

LetterOne . . . Company that includes Petr Aven and Richard Burt as board members. During a board meeting in December

2016, Aven asked for Burt's help to make contact with the Presidential Transition Team.

Link Campus University . . . University in Rome, Italy, where George Papadopoulos was introduced to Joseph Mifsud.

London Centre of International Law Practice (LCILP) . . . International law advisory organization in London that employed Joseph Mifsud and George Papadopoulos.

Main Intelligence Directorate of the General Staff (GRU) . . . Russian Federation's military intelligence agency.

New Economic School in Moscow (NES) . . . Moscow-based school that invited Carter Page to speak at its July 2016 commencement ceremony.

Opposition Bloc . . . Ukrainian political party that incorporated members of the defunct Party of Regions.

Party of Regions . . . Ukrainian political party of former President Yanukovych. It was generally understood to align with Russian policies.

Pericles Emerging Market Partners LLP . . . Company registered in the Cayman Islands by Paul Manafort and his business partner Rick Davis. Oleg Deripaska invested in the fund.

Prevezon Holdings Ltd. . . . Russian company that was a defendant in a U.S. civil action alleging the laundering of proceeds from fraud exposed by Sergei Magnitsky.

Roscongress Foundation . . . Russian entity that organized the St. Petersburg International Economic Forum.

Rosneft . . . Russian state-owned oil and energy company.

Russian Direct Investment Fund . . . Sovereign wealth fund established by the Russian Government in 2011 and headed by Kirill Dmitriev.

Russian International Affairs Council . . . Russia-based nonprofit established by Russian government decree. It is associated with the Ministry of Foreign Affairs, and its members include Ivan Timofeev, Dmitry Peskov, and Petr Aven.

Silk Road Group . . . Privately held investment company that entered into a licensing agreement to build a Trump-branded hotel in Georgia.

St. Petersburg International Economic Forum . . . Annual event held in Russia and attended by prominent Russian politicians and businessmen.

Tatneft . . . Russian energy company.

Transatlantic Parliamentary Group on Counterterrorism . . . European group that sponsored a summit between European Parliament lawmakers and U.S. persons. George Papadopoulos, Sam Clovis, and Walid Phares attended the TAG summit in July 2016.

Unit 26165 (GRU) . . . GRU military cyber unit dedicated to targeting military, political, governmental, and non-governmental organizations outside of Russia. It engaged in computer intrusions of U.S. persons and organizations, as well as the subsequent release of the stolen data, in order to interfere in the 2016 U.S. presidential election.

Unit 74455 (GRU) . . . GRU military unit with multiple departments that engaged in cyber operations. It engaged in computer intrusions of U.S. persons and organizations, as well as the subsequent release of the stolen data, in order to interfere in the 2016 U.S. presidential election.

Valdai Discussion Club . . . Group that holds a conference attended by Russian government officials, including President Putin.

WikiLeaks . . . Organization founded by Julian Assange that posts information online, including data stolen from private, corporate, and U.S. Government entities. Released data stolen by the GRU during the 2016 U.S. presidential election.

Index of Acronyms

CNI . . . Center for the National Interest

DCCC . . . Democratic Congressional Campaign Committee

DNC . . .Democratic National Committee

FBI . . . Federal Bureau of Investigation

FSB . . . Russian Federal Security Service

GEC . . . Global Energy Capital, LLC

GRU . . . Russian Federation's Main Intelligence Directorate of the General Staff

HPSCI . . . U.S. House of Representatives Permanent Select Committee on Intelligence

HRC . . . Hillary Rodham Clinton

IRA . . . Internet Research Agency

LCILP . . . London Centre of International Law Practice

NATO . . . North Atlantic Treaty Organization

NES . . . New Economic School

NSA . . . National Security Agency

ODNI . . . Office of the Director of National Intelligence

PTT . . . Presidential Transition Team

RDIF . . . Russian Direct Investment Fund

RIAC . . . Russian International Affairs Council

SBOE . . . State boards of elections

SCO . . . Special Counsel's Office

SJC . . . U.S. Senate Judiciary Committee

SSCI . . . U.S. Senate Select Committee on Intelligence

TAG . . . Transatlantic Parliamentary Group on Counterterrorism

VEB . . . Vnesheconombank

Appendix C

INTRODUCTORY NOTE

The President provided written responses through his personal counsel to questions submitted to him by the Special Counsel's Office. We first explain the process that led to the submission of written questions and then attach the President's responses.

Beginning in December 2017, this Office sought for more than a year to interview the President on topics relevant to both Russian-election interference and obstruction-of-justice. We advised counsel that the President was a "subject" of the investigation under the definition of the Justice Manual—"a person whose conduct is within the scope of the grand jury's investigation." Justice Manual & 9-11.151 (2018). We also advised counsel that "[a]n interview with the President is vital to our investigation" and that this Office had "carefully considered the constitutional and other arguments raised by ... counsel, and they d[id] not provide us with reason to forgo seeking an interview." We additionally stated that "it is in the interest of the Presidency and the public for an interview to take place" and offered "numerous accommodations to aid the President's preparation and avoid surprise." After extensive discussions with the Department of Justice about the Special Counsel's objective of securing the President's testimony, these accommodations included the submissions of written questions to the President on certain Russia-related topics.

We received the President's written responses in late November 2018. In December 2018, we informed counsel of the insufficiency of those responses in several respects. We noted, among other things, that the President stated on more than 30 occasions that he "does not recall' or 'remember' or have an 'independent recollection'" of information called for by the questions. Other answers were "incomplete or imprecise." The written responses, we informed counsel, "demonstrate the inadequacy of the written format, as we have had no opportunity to ask follow-up questions that would ensure complete answers and potentially refresh your client's recollection or clarify the extent or nature of his lack of recollection." We again requested an in-person interview, limited to certain topics, advising the President's counsel that "[t]his is the President's

5/16/18 Letter, Special Counsel to the President's Personal Counsel, at 1.

5/16/18 Letter, Special Counsels's Office to the President's Personal Counsel, at 1; see 7/30/18 Letter, Special Counsel's Office to the President's Personal Counsel, at 1 (describing accommodations).

Letter, Special Counsel's Office to the President's Personal Counsel, at 1 (submitting written questions).

11/20/18 Letter, President's Personal Counsel to the Special Counsel's Office (transmitting written responses of Donald J. Trump).

12/3/18 Letter, Special Counsel's Office to the President's Personal Counsel, at 3.

12/3/18 Letter, Special Counsel's Office to the President's Personal Counsel, at 3.

12/3/18 Letter, Special Counsel's Office to the President's Personal Counsel, at 3; see (noting, "for example," that the President "did not answer whether he had at any time directed or suggested that discussions about the Trump Moscow Project should cease ... but he has since made public comments about that topic").

12/3/18 Letter, Special Counsel's Office to the President's Personal Counsel, at 3.

opportunity to voluntarily provide us with information for us to evaluate in the context of all of the evidence we have gathered." The President declined.

Recognizing that the President would not be interviewed voluntarily, we considered whether to issue a subpoena for his testimony. We viewed the written answers to be inadequate. But at that point, our investigation had made significant progress and had produced substantial evidence for our report. We thus weighed the costs of potentially lengthy constitutional litigation, with resulting delay in finishing our investigation, against the anticipated benefits for our investigation and report. As explained in Volume II, Section II.B., we determined that the substantial quantity of information we had obtained from other sources allowed us to draw relevant factual conclusions on intent and credibility, which are often inferred from circumstantial evidence and assessed without direct testimony from the subject of the investigation.

*   *   *

12/3/18 Letter, Special Counsel to the President's Personal Counsel.

12/12/18 Letter, President's Personal Counsel to the Special Counsel's Office, at 2.

WRITTEN QUESTIONS TO BE ANSWERED UNDER OATH BY PRESIDENT DONALD J. TRUMP

I. June 9, 2016 Meeting at Trump Tower

Parts (a, b, & c)

a. When did you first learn that Donald Trump, Jr., Paul Manafort, or Jared Kushner was considering participating in a meeting in June 2016 concerning potentially negative information about Hillary Clinton? Describe who you learned the information from and the substance of the discussion.

b. Attached to this document as Exhibit A is a series of emails from June 2016 between, among others, Donald Trump, Jr. and Rob Goldstone. In addition to the emails reflected in Exhibit A, Donald Trump, Jr. had other communications with Rob Goldstone and Emin Agalarov between June 3, 2016, and June 9, 2016.

i. Did Mr. Trump, Jr. or anyone else tell you about or show you any of these communications? If yes, describe who discussed the communications with you, when, and the substance of the discussion(s).

ii. When did you first see or learn about all or any part of the emails reflected in Exhibit A?

iii. When did you first learn that the proposed meeting involved or was described as being part of Russia and its government's support for your candidacy?

iv. Did you suggest to or direct anyone not to discuss or release publicly all or any portion of the emails reflected in Exhibit A?

If yes, describe who you communicated with, when, the substance of the communication(s), and why you took that action.

c. On June 9, 2016, Donald Trump, Jr., Paul Manafort, and Jared Kushner attended a meeting at Trump Tower with several individuals, including a Russian lawyer, Natalia Veselnitskaya (the "June 9 meeting").

i. Other than as set forth in your answers to I.a and 1.b, what, if anything, were you told about the possibility of this meeting taking place, or the scheduling of such a meeting? Describe who you discussed this with, when, and what you were informed about the meeting.

ii. When did you learn that some of the individuals attending the June 9 meeting were Russian or had any affiliation with any part of the Russian government? Describe who you learned this information from and the substance of the discussion(s).

iii. What were you told about what was discussed at the June 9 meeting? Describe each conversation in which you were told about what was discussed at the meeting, who the conversation was with, when it occurred, and the substance of the statements they made about the meeting.

iv. Were you told that the June 9 meeting was about, in whole or in part, adoption and/or the Magnitsky Act? If yes, describe who you had that discussion with, when, and the substance of the discussion.

Response to Question l, Parts (a), (b), & (c)

I have no recollection of learning at the time that Donald Trump, Jr., Paul Manafort, or Jared Kushner was considering participating in a meeting in June 2016 concerning potentially negative information about Hillary Clinton. Nor do I recall learning during the campaign that the June 9, 2016 meeting had taken place, that the referenced emails existed. or that Donald J. Trump, Jr., had other communications with Emin Agalarov or Robert Goldstone between June 3, 2016 and June 9, 2016.

Part (d)

d. For the period June 6, 2016 through June 9, 2016, for what portion of each day were you in Trump Tower?

i. Did you speak or meet with Donald Trump, Jr., Paul Manafort, or Jared Kushner on June 9, 2016? If yes, did any portion of any of those conversations or meetings include any reference to any aspect of the June 9 meeting? If yes, describe who you spoke with and the substance of the conversation.

Response to Question I, Part (d)

I have no independent recollection of what portion of these four days in June of 2016 I spent in Trump Tower. This was one of many busy months during a fast-paced campaign, as the primary season was ending and we were preparing for the general election campaign.

I am now aware that my Campaign's calendar indicates that I was in New York City from June 6 - 9, 2016. Calendars kept in my Trump Tower office reflect that I had various calls and meetings scheduled for each of these days. While those calls and meetings may or may not actually have taken place, they do indicate that I was in Trump Tower during a portion of each of these working days, and I have no reason to doubt that I was. When I was in New York City, I stayed at my Trump Tower apartment.

My Trump Organization desk calendar also reflects that I was outside Trump Tower during portions of these days. The June 7, 2016 calendar indicates I was scheduled to leave Trump Tower in the early evening for Westchester where I gave remarks after winning the California, New Jersey, New Mexico, Montana, and South Dakota Republican primaries held that day. The June 8, 2016 calendar indicates a scheduled departure in late afternoon to attend a ceremony at my son's school. The June 9, 2016 calendar indicates I was scheduled to attend midday meetings and a fundraising luncheon at the Four Seasons Hotel. At this point, I do not remember on what dales these events occurred, but I do not currently have a reason to doubt that they took place as scheduled on my calendar.

Widely available media reports, including television footage, also shed light on my activities during these days. For example, I am aware that my June 7, 2016 victory remarks at the Trump National Golf Club in Briarcliff Manor, New York, were recorded and published by the media. I remember winning those primaries and generally recall delivering remarks that evening.

At this point in time, I do not remember whether I spoke or met with Donald Trump, Jr., Paul Manafort, or Jared Kushner on June 9, 2016. My desk calendar indicates I was scheduled to meet with Paul Manafort on the morning of June 9, but I do not recall if that meeting took place. It was more than two years ago, at a time when I had many calls and interactions daily.

Part (e)

e. Did you communicate directly or indirectly with any member or representative of the Agalarov family after June 3, 2016? If yes, describe who you spoke with, when, and the substance of the communication.

Response to Question I, Part (e)

I have no independent recollection of any communications I had with the Agalarov family or anyone r understood to be a representative of the Agalarov family after June 3, 2016 and before the end of the campaign. While preparing to respond to these questions, I have become aware of written communications with the Agalarovs during the campaign that were sent, received, and largely authored by my staff and which I understand have already been produced to you.

In general, the documents include congratulatory letters on my campaign victories, emails about a painting Emin and Aras Agalarov arranged to have delivered to Trump Tower as a birthday present, and emails regarding delivery of a book written by Aras Agalarov. The documents reflect that the deliveries were screened by the Secret Service.

Part (f)

f. Did you learn of any communications between Donald Trump, Jr., Paul Manafort, or Jared Kushner and any member or representative of the Agalarov family, Natalia Veselnitskaya, Rob Goldstone, or any Russian official or contact that took place after June 9, 2016 and concerned the June 9 meeting or efforts by Russia to assist the campaign? If yes, describe who you learned this information from, when, and the substance of what you learned.

Response to Question I, Part (f)

I do not recall being aware during the campaign of communications between Donald Trump, Jr., Paul Manafort, or Jared Kushner and any member or representative of the Agalarov family, Robert Goldstone, Natalia Yeselnitskaya (whose name I was not familiar with), or anyone I understood to be a Russian official.

Part (g)

g. On June 7, 2016, you gave a speech in which you said, in part, "I am going to give a major speech on probably Monday of next week and we're going to be discussing all of the things that have taken place with the Clintons."

i. Why did you make that statement?

ii. What information did you plan to share with respect to the Clintons?

iii. What did you believe the source(s) of that information would be?

iv. Did you expect any of the information to have come from the June 9 meeting?

v. Did anyone help draft the speech that you were referring to? If so, who?

vi. Why did you ultimately not give the speech you referenced on June 7, 2016?

Response to Question I, Part (g)

In remarks I delivered the night I won the California, New Jersey, New Mexico, Montana, and South Dakota Republican primaries, I said, "I am going to give a major speech on probably Monday of next week and we're going to be discussing all of the things that have taken place with the Clintons." In general, I expected to give a speech referencing the publicly available, negative information about the Clintons, including, for example, Mrs. Clinton's failed policies, the Clintons' use of the State Department to further their interests and the interests of the Clinton Foundation, Mrs. Clinton's improper use of a private server for State Department business, the destruction of 33,000 emails on that server, and Mrs. Clinton's temperamental unsuitability for the office of President.

In the course of preparing to respond to your questions, I have become aware that the Campaign documents already produced to you reflect the drafting, evolution, and sources of information for the speech I expected to give "probably" on the Monday fol lowing my June 7, 2016 comments. These documents generally show that the text of the speech was initially drafted by Campaign staff with input from various outside advisors and was based on publicly available material, including, in particular, information from the book *Clinton Cash* by Peter Schweizer.

The Pulse Nightclub terrorist attack took place in the early morning hours of Sunday, June 12, 2016. In light of that tragedy, I gave a speech directed more specifically to national security and terrorism than to the Clintons. That speech was delivered at the Saint Anselm College Institute of Politics in Manchester, New Hampshire, and, as reported, opened with the following:

This was going to be a speech on Hillary Clinton and how bad a President, especially in these times of Radical Islamic Terrorism, she would be. Even her former Secret Service Agent, who has seen her under pressure and in times of stress, has stated that she lacks the temperament and integrity to be president. There will be plenty of oppoltunity to discuss these important issues at a later time, and I will deliver that speech soon. But today there is only one thing to discuss: the growing threat of terrorism inside of our borders.

I continued to speak about Mrs. Clinton's failings throughout the campaign, using the information prepared for inclusion in the speech to which I referred on June 7, 2016.

Part (h)

h. Did any person or entity inform you during the campaign that Vladimir Putin or the Russian government supported your candidacy or opposed the candidacy of Hillary Clinton? If yes,describe the source(s) of the information. when you were informed, and the content of such discussion(s).

Response to Question I, Part (h)

I have no recollection of being told during the campaign that Vladimir Putin or the Russian government "suppotted" my candidacy or "opposed" the candidacy of Hillary Clinton. However, I was aware of some reports indicating that President Putin had made complimentary statements about me.

Part (i)

i. Did any person or entity inform you during the campaign that any foreign government or foreign leader, other than Russia or Vladimir Putin, had provided, wished to provide, or offered to provide tangible support to your campaign, including by way of offering to provide negative information on Hillary Clinton? If yes, describe the source{s) of the information, when you were informed, and the content of such discussion(s).

Response to Question I, Part (i)

I have no recollection of being told during the campaign that any foreign government or foreign leader had provided, wished to provide, or offered to provide tangible support to my campaign.

II. Russian Hacking/ Russian Efforts Using Social Media / Wikileaks

Part (a)

a. On June 14, 2016, it was publicly reported that computer hackers had penetrated the computer network of the Democratic National Committee {DNC) and that Russian intelligence was behind the unauthorized access, or hack. Prior to June 4, 2016, were you provided any information about any potential or actual hacking of the computer systems or email accounts of the DNC, the Democratic Congressional Campaign Committee (DCCC), the Clinton Campaign, Hillary Clinton, or individuals associated with the Clinton campaign? If yes, describe who provided this information, when, and the substance of the information.

Response to Question II, Part (a)

I do not remember the date on which it was publicly reported that the DNC had been hacked, but my best recollection is that I learned of the hacking at or shortly after the time it became the subject of media reporting. I do not recall being provided any information during the campaign about the hacking of any of the named entities or individuals before it became the subject of media reporting.

Part (b)

b. On July 22, 2016, Wikileaks released nearly 20,000 emails sent or received by Democratic party officials.

i. Prior to the July 22, 2016 release, were you aware from any source that Wikileaks, Guccifer 2.0, DCLeaks, or Russians had or potentially had possession of or planned to release emails or information that could help your campaign or hurt the Clinton campaign? If yes, describe who you discussed this issue with, when, and the substance of the discussion(s).

ii. After the release of emails by Wikileaks on July 22, 2016, were you told that Wikileaks possessed or might possess additional information that could be released during the campaign? If yes, describe who provided this information, when, and what you were told.

Response to Question II, Part (b)

I recall that in the months leading up to the election there was considerable media reporting about the possible hacking and release of campaign-related information and there was a lot of talk about this matter. At the time, I was generally aware of these media reports and may have discussed these issues with my campaign staff or others, but at this point in time - more than two years later - I have no recollection of any particular conversation, when it occurred, or who the participants were.

Part (c)

c. Are you aware of any communications during the campaign, directly or indirectly, between Roger Stone, Donald Trump, Jr., Paul Manafort, or Rick Gates and {a} Wikileaks, {b} Julian Assange, (c) other representatives of Wikileaks, {d} Guccifer 2.0, (e) representatives of Guccifer 2.0, or {f} representatives of DCLeaks? If yes, describe who provided you with this information, when you learned of the communications, and what you know about those communications.

Response to Question II, Part (c)

I do not recall being aware during the campaign of any communications between the individuals named in Question II (c) and anyone I understood to be a representative of WikiLeaks or any of the other individuals or entities referred to in the question.

Part (d)

d. On July 27, 2016, you stated at a press conference: "Russia, if you're listening, I hope you're able to find the 30,000 emails that are missing. I think you will probably be rewarded mightily by our press."

i. Why did you make that request of Russia, as opposed to any other country, entity, or individual?

ii. In advance of making that statement, what discussions, if any, did you have with anyone else about the substance of the statement?

iii. Were you told at any time before or after you made that statement that Russia was attempting to infiltrate or hack computer systems or email accounts of Hillary Clinton or her campaign? If yes, describe who provided this information, when, and what you were told.

Response to Question II, Part (d)

I made the statement quoted in Question II (d) in jest and sarcastically, as was apparent to any objective observer. The context of the statement is evident in the full reading or viewing of the July 27, 2016 press conference, and I refer you to the publicly available transcript and video of that press conference. I do not recall having any discussion about the substance of the statement in advance of the press conference. I do not recall being told during the campaign of any efforts by

Russia to infiltrate or hack the computer systems or email accounts of Hillary Clinton or her campaign prior to them becoming the subject of media repolling and I have no recollection of any particular conversation in that regard.

Part (e)

e. On October 7, 2016, emails hacked from the account of John Podesta were released by WikiLeaks.

i. Where were you on October 7, 2016?

ii. Were you told at any time in advance of, or on the day of, the October 7 release that Wikileaks possessed or might possess emails related to John Podesta? If yes, describe who told you this, when, and what you were told.

iii. Are you aware of anyone associated with you or your campaign, including Roger Stone, reaching out to Wikileaks, either directly or through an intermediary, on or about October 7, 2016? If yes, identify the person and describe the substance of the conversations or contacts.

Response to Question II, Part (e)

I was in Trump Tower in New York City on October 7, 2016. I have no recollection of being told that WikiLeaks possessed or might possess emails related to John Podesta before the release of Mr. Podesta's emails was reported by the media. Likewise, I have no recollection of being told that Roger Stone, anyone acting as an intermediary for Roger Stone, or anyone associated with my campaign had communicated with WikiLeaks on October 7, 2016.

Part (f)

f. Were you told of anyone associated with you or your campaign, including Roger Stone, having any discussions, directly or indirectly, with Wikileaks, Guccifer 2.0, or DCLeaks regarding the content or timing of release of hacked emails? If yes, describe who had such contacts, how you became aware of the contacts, when you became aware of the contacts, and the substance of the contacts.

Response to Question II, Part (f)

I do not recall being told during the campaign that Roger Stone or anyone associated with my campaign had discussions with any of the entities named in the question regarding the content or timing of release of hacked emails.

Part (g)

g. From June 1, 2016 through the end of the campaign, how frequently did you communicate with Roger Stone? Describe the nature of your communication(s) with Mr. Stone.

i. During that time period, what efforts did Mr. Stone tell you he was making to assist your campaign, and what requests, if any, did you make of Mr. Stone?

ii. Did Mr. Stone ever discuss Wikileaks with you or, as far as you were aware, with anyone else associated with the campaign? If yes, describe what you were told, from whom, and when.

iii. Did Mr. Stone at any time inform you about contacts he had with Wikileaks or any intermediary of WikiLeaks, or about forthcoming releases of information? If yes, describe what Stone told you and when.

Response to Question II, Part (g)

I spoke by telephone with Roger Stone from time to time during the campaign. I have no recollection of the specifics of any conversations I had with Mr. Stone between June 1.2016 and November 8, 2016. I do not recall discussing WikiLeaks with him, nor do I recall being aware of Mr. Stone having discussed WikiLeaks with individuals associated with my campaign, although I was aware that WikiLeaks was the subject of media reporting and campaign-related discussion at the time.

Part (h)

h. Did you have any discussions prior to January 20, 2017, regarding a potential pardon or other action to benefit Julian Assange? If yes, describe who you had the discussion(s) with, when, and the content of the discussion(s).

Response to Question II, Part (h)

I do not recall having had any discussion during the campaign regarding a pardon or action to benefit Julian Assange.

Part (i)

i. Were you aware of any efforts by foreign individuals or companies, including those in Russia, to assist your campaign through the use of social media postings or the organization of rallies? If yes, identify who you discussed such assistance with, when, and the content of the discussion(s).

Response to Question II, Part (i)

I do not recall being aware during the campaign of specific efforts by foreign individuals or companies to assist my campaign through the use of social media postings or the organization of rallies.

III. The Trump Organization Moscow Project

Parts (a through g)

a. In October 2015, a "Letter of Intent," a copy of which is attached as Exhibit B, was signed for a proposed Trump Organization project in Moscow (the "Trump Moscow project").

i. When were you first informed of discussions about the Trump Moscow project? By whom? What were you told about the project?

ii. Did you sign the letter of intent?

b. In a statement provided to Congress, attached as Exhibit C, Michael Cohen stated: "To the best of my knowledge, Mr. Trump was never in contact with anyone about this proposal other than me on three occasions, including signing a non-binding letter of intent in 2015." Describe all discussions you had with Mr. Cohen, or anyone else associated with the Trump

Organization, about the Trump Moscow project, including who you spoke with, when, and the substance of the discussion(s).

c. Did you learn of any communications between Michael Cohen or Felix Sater and any Russian government officials, including officials in the office of Dmitry Peskov, regarding the Trump Moscow project? If so, identify who provided this information to you, when, and the substance of what you learned.

d. Did you have any discussions between June 2015 and June 2016 regarding a potential trip to Russia by you and/or Michael Cohen for reasons related to the Trump Moscow project? If yes, describe who you spoke with, when, and the substance of the discussion(s).

e. Did you at any time direct or suggest that discussions about the Trump Moscow project should cease, or were you informed at any time that the project had been abandoned? If yes, describe who you spoke with, when, the substance of the discussion(s), and why that decision was made.

f. Did you have any discussions regarding what information would be provided publicly or in response to investigative inquiries about potential or actual investments or business deals the Trump Organization had in Russia, including the Trump

C-26

Moscow project? If yes, describe who you spoke with, when, and the substance of the discussion(s).

g. Aside from the Trump Moscow project, did you or the Trump Organization have any other prospective or actual business interests, investments, or arrangements with Russia or any Russian interest or Russian individual during the campaign? If yes, describe the business interests, investments, or arrangements.

Response to Question III, Parts (a through g)

Sometime in 2015, Michael Cohen suggested to me the possibility of a Trump Organization project in Moscow. As I recall, Mr. Cohen described this as a proposed project of a general type we have done in the past in a variety of locations. I signed the non-binding Letter of Intent attached to your questions as Exhibit B which required no equity or expenditure on our end and was consistent with our ongoing efforts to expand into significant markets around the world.

I had few conversations with Mr. Cohen on this subject. As I recall, they were brief, and they were not memorable. I was not enthused about the proposal, and 1 do not recall any discussion of travel to Russia in connection with it. I do not remember discussing it with anyone else at the Trump Organization, although it is possible. I do not recall being aware at the time of any communications between Mr. Cohen or Felix Sater and any Russian government official regarding the Letter of Intent. In the course of preparing to respond to your questions, I have become aware that Mr. Cohen sent an email regarding the Letter of Intent to "Mr. Peskov" at a general, public email account, which should show there was no meaningful relationship with people in power in Russia. I understand those documents already have been provided to you.

I vaguely remember press inquiries and media reporting during the campaign about whether the Trump Organization had business dealings in Russia. I may have spoken with campaign staff or Trump Organization employees regarding responses to requests for information, but 1 have no current recollection of any particular conversation, with whom I may have spoken, when, or the substance of any conversation. As I recall , neither I nor the Trump Organization had any projects or proposed projects in Russia during the campaign other than the Letter of Intent.

IV. Contacts with Russia and Russia-Related Issues During the Campaign

Parts (a through d)

a. Prior to mid-August 2016, did you become aware that Paul Manafort had ties to the Ukrainian government? If yes, describe who you learned this information from, when, and the substance of what you were told. Did Mr. Manafort's connections to the Ukrainian or Russian governments play any role in your decision to have him join your campaign? If yes, describe that role.

b. Were you aware that Paul Manafort offered briefings on the progress of your campaign to Oleg Deripaska? If yes, describe who you learned this information from , when, the substance of what you were told, what you understood the purpose was of sharing such information with Mr. Deripaska, and how you responded to learning this information.

c. Were you aware of whether Paul Manafort or anyone else associated with your campaign sent or directed others to send internal Trump campaign information to any person located in Ukraine or Russia or associated with the Ukrainian or Russian governments? If yes, identify who provided you with this information, when, the substance of the discussion(s), what you understood the purpose was of sharing the internal campaign information, and how you responded to learning this information.

d. Did Paul Manafort communicate to you, directly or indirectly. any positions Ukraine or Russia would want the U.S. to support? If yes, describe when he communicated those positions to you and the substance of those communications.

Response to Question IV, Parts (a through d)

Mr. Manafort was hired primarily because of his delegate work for prior presidential candidates, including Gerald Ford, Ronald Reagan, George H.W. Bush, and Bob Dole. I knew that Mr. Manafort had done international consulting work and, at some time before Mr. Manafort left the campaign, I learned that he was somehow involved with individuals concerning Ukraine, but I do not remember the specifics of what I knew at the time.

I had no knowledge of Mr. Manafort offering briefings on the progress of my campaign to an individual named Oleg Deripaska, nor do I remember being aware of Mr. Manafort or anyone else associated with my campaign sending or directing others to send internal Trump Campaign information to anyone I knew to be in Ukraine or Russia at the time or to anyone I understood to be a Ukrainian or Russian government employee or official. I do not remember Mr. Manafort communicating to me any particular positions Ukraine or Russia would want the United States to support.

Part (e)

e. During the campaign, were you told about efforts by Russian officials to meet with you or senior members of your campaign? If yes, describe who you had conversations with on this topic, when, and what you were told.

Response to Question IV, Part (e)

I do not recall being told during the campaign of efforts by Russian officials to meet with me or with senior members of my campaign. In the process of preparing to respond to these questions, I became aware that on March 17, 2016, my assistant at the Trump Organization, Rhona Graff, received an email from a Sergei Prikhodko, who identified himself as Deputy Prime Minister of the Russian Federation, Foundation Roscongress, inviting me to participate in the St. Petersburg International Economic Forum to be held in June 2016. The documents show that Ms. Graff prepared for my signature a brief response declining the invitation. I understand these documents already have been produced to you.

Part (f)

f. What role, if any, did you have in changing the Republican Party platform regarding arming Ukraine during the Republican National Convention? Prior to the convention, what information did you have about this platform provision? After the platform provision was changed, who told you about the change, when did they tell you, what were you told about why it was changed, and who was involved?

Response to Question IV, Part (f)

I have no recollection of the details of what, when, or from what source I first learned about the change to the platform amendment regarding arming Ukraine, but I generally recall learning of the issue as pa1t of media reporting. I do not recall being involved in changing the language to the amendment.

Part (g)

g. On July 27, 2016, in response to a question about whether you would recognize Crimea as Russian territory and lift sanctions on Russia, you said: "We'll be looking at that. Yeah, we'll be looking." Did you intend to communicate by that statement or at any other time during the campaign a willingness to lift sanctions and/or recognize Russia's annexation of Crimea if you were elected?

i. What consideration did you give to lifting sanctions and/or recognizing Russia's annexation of Crimea if you were elected? Describe who you spoke with about this topic, when, the substance of the discussion(s).

Response to Question IV, Part (g)

My statement did not communicate any position.

V. Contacts with Russia and Russia-Related Issues During the Transition

Part (a)

a. Were you asked to attend the World Chess Championship gala on November 10, 2016? If yes, who asked you to attend, when were you asked, and what were you told about about [sic] why your presence was requested?

i. Did you attend any part of the event? If yes, describe any interactions you had with any Russians or representatives of the Russian government at the event.

V. Contacts with Russia and Russia-Related Issues During the Transition

Part (a)

a. Were you asked to attend the World Chess Championship gala on November 10, 2016? If yes, who asked you to attend, when were you asked, and what were you told about about why your presence was requested?

Response to Question V, Part (a)

I do not remember having been asked to attend the World Chess Championship gala, and I did not attend the event. During the course of preparing to respond to these questions, I have become aware of documents indicating that in March of 2016, the president of the World Chess Federation invited the Trump Organization to host, at Trump Tower, the 2016 World Chess Championship Match to be held in New York in November 2016. I have also become aware that in November 2016, there were press inquiries to my staff regarding whether I had plans to attend the tournament, which was not being held at Trump Tower. I understand these documents have already been provided to you.

Executed on *NOVEMBER **20**,* 2018

Donald J. Trump
President of the United States

Appendix D

APPENDIX D

SPECIAL COUNSEL'S OFFICE TRANSFERRED, REFERRED, AND COMPLETED CASES

This appendix identifies matters transferred or referred by the Special Counsel's Office, as well as cases prosecuted by the Office that are now completed.

A. Transfers

The Special Counsel's Office has concluded its investigation into links and coordination between the Russian government and individuals associated with the Trump Campaign. Certain matters assigned to the Office by the Acting Attorney General have not fully concluded as of the date of this report. After consultation with the Office of the Deputy Attorney General, the Office has transferred responsibility for those matters to other components of the Department of Justice and the FBI. Those transfers include:

1. <u>United States v. Bijan Rafiekian and Kami! Ekim Alptekin</u>

US. Attorney's Office for the Eastern District of Virginia (Awaiting trial)

The Acting Attorney General authorized the Special Counsel to investigate, among other things, possible criminal conduct by Michael Flynn in acting as an unregistered agent for the Government of Turkey. See August 2, 2017 Memorandum from Rod J. Rosenstein to Robert S. Mueller, III. The Acting Attorney General later confirmed the Special Counsel's authority to investigate Rafiekian and Alptekin because they "may have been jointly involved" with Flynn in FARA-related crimes. See October 20, 2017 Memorandum from Associate Deputy Attorney General Scott Schools to Deputy Attorney General Rod J. Rosenstein.

On December 1, 2017, Flynn pleaded guilty to an Information charging him with making false statements to the FBI about his contacts with the Russian ambassador to the United States. As part of that plea, Flynn agreed to a Statement of the Offense in which he acknowledged that the Foreign Agents Registration Act (FARA) documents he filed on March 7, 2017 "contained materially false statements and omissions." Flynn's plea occurred before the Special Counsel had made a final decision on whether to charge Rafiekian or Alptekin. On March 27, 2018, after consultation with the Office of the Deputy Attorney General, the Special Counsel' s Office referred the investigation of Rafiekian and Alptekin to the National Security Division (NSD) for any action it deemed appropriate. The Special Counsel's Office determined the referral was appropriate because the investigation of Flynn had been completed, and that investigation had provided the rationale for the Office's investigation of Rafiekian and Alptekin. At NS D's request, the Eastern District of Virginia continued the investigation of Rafiekian and Alptekin.

2. United States v. Michael Flynn

US. Attorney's Office for the District of Columbia (A waiting sentencing)

3. United States v. Richard Gates

U.S. Attorney's Office for the District of Columbia (Awaiting sentencing)

4. United States v. Internet Research Agency, et al (Russian Social Media Campaign)

U.S. Attorney's Office for the District of Columbia

National Security Division

(Post-indictment, pre-arrest & pre-trial)

5. United States v. Konstantin Kilimnik

U.S. Attorney's Office for the District of Columbia (Post-indictment, pre-arrest)

6. <u>United States v. Paul Manafort</u>

U.S. Attorney's Office for the District of Columbia

U.S. Attorney's Office for the Eastern District of Virginia (Post-conviction)

7. <u>United States v. Viktor Netyksho, et al.</u> (Russian Hacking Operations)

U.S. Attorney's Office for the Western District of Pennsylvania

National Security Division (Post-indictment, pre-arrest)

8. <u>United States v. William Samuel Patten</u>

U.S. Attorney's Office for the District of Columbia (Awaiting sentencing)

The Acting Attorney General authorized the Special Counsel to investigate aspects of Patten's conduct that related to another matter that was under investigation by the Office. The investigation uncovered evidence of a crime; the U.S.

Attorney's Office for the District of Columbia handled the prosecution of Patten.

9. ██

████████████████████████████(Investigation ongoing)

The Acting Attorney General authorized the Special Counsel to investigate, among other things, crime or crimes arising out of payments Paul Manafort received from the Ukrainian government before and during the tenure of President Viktor Yanukovych. See August 2, 2017 Memorandum from Rod J. Rosenstein to Robert S. Mueller, III. The Acting Attorney General

One defendant, Concord Management & Consulting LLC, appeared through counsel and is in pretrial litigation.

later confirmed the Special Counsel's authority to investigate

██

██

██

██

██

██

On October 27, 2017, Paul Manafort and Richard Gates were charged in the District of Columbia with various crimes (including FARA) in connection with work they performed for Russia-backed political entities in Ukraine. On February 22, 2018, Manafort and Gates were charged in the Eastern District of Virginia with various other crimes in connection with the payments they received for work performed for Russia-backed political entities in Ukraine. During the course of its ▆▆▆▆▆▆▆▆ the Special Counsel's Office developed substantial evidence with respect to individuals and entities that wer ▆▆▆▆▆▆▆

▆▆▆▆▆▆▆▆▆▆▆▆. On February 23, 2018, Gates pleaded guilty in the District of Columbia to a multi-object conspiracy and to making false statements; the remaining charges against Gates were dismissed. Thereafter, in consultation with the Office of the Deputy Attorney General, the Special Counsel's Office closed the ███ and referred ███████████████████████████████████████ them ███

███

███

████████████████████████ for further investigation as it deemed appropriate. The Office based its decision to close those matters on its mandate, the indictments of Manafort, Gates's plea, and its determination as to how best to allocate its resources, among other reasons; ███

███

███

█████████████████████ At ███

███████████████████████████████████████ continued the investigation of those closed matters.

10. <u>United States v. Roger Stone</u>

U.S. Attorney's Office for the District of Columbia (Awaiting trial)

11. ██

██

██

████████████████████████████████(Investigation ongoing)

B. Referrals

During the course of the investigation, the Office periodically identified evidence of potential criminal activity that was outside the scope of the Special Counsel's jurisdiction established by the Acting Attorney General. After consultation with the Office of the Deputy Attorney General, the Office referred that evidence to appropriate law enforcement authorities, principally other components of the Department of Justice and the FBI. Those referrals, listed

██

██

██

██

██

██

██████████████████████████████████████

Manafort was ultimately convicted at trial in the Eastern District of Virginia and pleaded guilty in the District of Columbia. See Vol. I, Section IV.A.8. The trial and plea happened after the transfer decision described here.

alphabetically by subject, are summarized below.

1. ██

██

██

██

██

██

██

██

2. <u>Michael Cohen</u>

During the course of the investigation, the Special Counsel's Office uncovered evidence of potential wire fraud and FECA violations pertaining to Michael Cohen. That evidence was referred to the U.S. Attorney's Office for the Southern District of New York and the FBI's New York Field Office.

3.

4.

5. Gregory Craig

██

██ Skadden, Arps, Slate, Meagher & Flom LLP

6. During the course of the FARA investigation of Paul Manafort and Rick Gates, the Special Counsel's Office uncovered evidence of potential FARA violations pertaining to

██

Gregory Craig, Skadden, Arps, Slate, Meagher & Flom LLP (Skadden), and their work on behalf of the government of Ukraine.

After consultation with the NSD, the evidence regarding Craig ██████████████████████████████ was referred to NSD, and NSD elected to partner with the U.S. Attorney's Office for the Southern District of New York and the FBI's New York Field Office. NSD later elected to partner on the Craig matter with the U.S. Attorney's Office for the District of Columbia. NSD retained and handled issues relating to Skadden itself.

6. ██████████████████████████████

D-14

7.

8.

9.

10.

11.

D-18

12.

13.

14.

██

██

C. Completed Prosecutions

In three cases prosecuted by the Special Counsel's Office, the defendants have completed or are about to complete their terms of imprisonment. Because no further proceedings are likely in any case, responsibility for them has not been transferred to any other office or component.

1. <u>United States v. George Papadopoulos</u>

Post-conviction, Completed term of imprisonment (December 7, 2018)

2. <u>United States v. Alex van der Zwaan</u>

Post-conviction, Completed term of imprisonment (June 4, 2018)

3. <u>United States v. Richard Pinedo</u>

Post-conviction, Currently in Residential Reentry Center (release date May 13, 2019)

000700027000061

Made in the USA
San Bernardino, CA
17 June 2019